ANCIENT ROME

BY DANIEL R. FAUST

Gareth Stevens
PUBLISHING

CRASHCOURSE

Please visit our website, www.garethstevens.com. For a free color catalog of all our high-quality books, call toll free 1-800-542-2595 or fax 1-877-542-2596.

Library of Congress Cataloging-in-Publication Data

Names: Faust, Daniel R., author.
Title: Ancient Rome / Daniel R. Faust.
Description: New York : Gareth Stevens Publishing, 2019. | Series: A look at ancient civilizations | Includes index.
Identifiers: LCCN 2018022957| ISBN 9781538230084 (library bound) | ISBN 9781538231647 (pbk.) | ISBN 9781538233276 (6 pack)
Subjects: LCSH: Rome--History--Juvenile literature. | Rome--Civilization--Juvenile literature.
Classification: LCC DG77 .F83 2019 | DDC 937--dc23
LC record available at https://lccn.loc.gov/2018022957

First Edition

Published in 2019 by
Gareth Stevens Publishing
111 East 14th Street, Suite 349
New York, NY 10003

Copyright © 2019 Gareth Stevens Publishing

Designer: Reann Nye
Editor: Tayler Cole

Photo credits: Series art (writing background) mcherevan/Shutterstock.com, (map) Andrey_Kuzmin/Shutterstock.com; cover, p. 1 givaga/Shutterstock.com; p. 5 mekcar/Shutterstock.com; p. 7 Skoda/Shutterstock.com; p. 9 Cris Foto/Shutterstock.com; p. 11 Stefano Bianchetti/Corbis Historical/Getty Images; p. 13 Brian Maudsley/Shutterstock.com; p. 15 ullstein bild Dtl./ullstein bild/Getty Images; p. 17 Viacheslav Lopatin/Shuttersrock.com; p. 19 Cortyn/Shutterstock.com; p. 21 Ray Wise/Moment/Getty Images; p. 23 Phant/Shutterstock.com; p. 25 koyash07/Shutterstock.com; p. 27 Highlywood Photography/Moment/Getty Images; p. 29 muratart/Shutterstock.com.

Printed in the United States of America

CPSIA compliance information: Batch #CW19GS: For further information contact Gareth Stevens, New York, New York at 1-800-542-2595.

CONTENTS

Words in the glossary appear in **bold** type the first time they are used in the text.

FROM VILLAGES TO A CITY

Rome began as several small villages built on hills near the Tiber River in Italy around 800 BC. These villages began to join together into a larger city in the 700s BC. Around 600 BC, the city of Rome was **conquered** by a group called the Etruscans.

Make The Grade

According to ancient stories, Rome was founded by twin brothers, Romulus and Remus. The brothers wanted to build a city, but they fought over where. Romulus killed Remus and named the city "Rome" after himself.

Tiber River

THE EARLY REPUBLIC

Rome was ruled by the Etruscans for about 100 years. The city grew and became very powerful in this time. In 509 BC, the Romans, led by Lucius Junius Brutus, overthrew the last Etruscan king. Rome then became a **republic**.

Make The Grade

The people of early Rome learned about trade from the Etruscans. They learned about **religion** and art from the Greeks who lived to the south.

Instead of a king, the Roman Republic had two consuls. These generals led the army during times of war. The consuls only served for a year, so they couldn't become too powerful. Together, they worked with hundreds of Senate members who served for life. The Senate was a governing body in Rome.

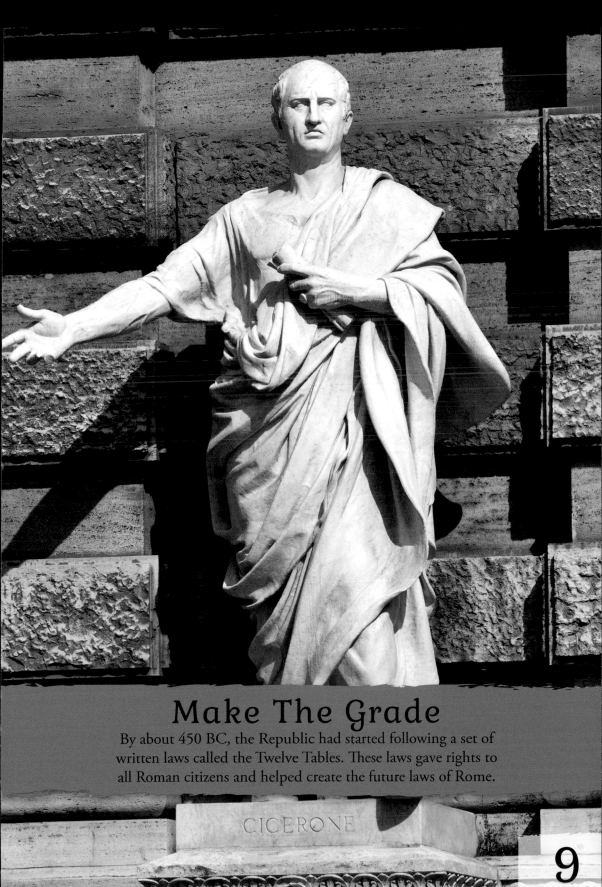

Make The Grade

By about 450 BC, the Republic had started following a set of written laws called the Twelve Tables. These laws gave rights to all Roman citizens and helped create the future laws of Rome.

CICERONE

9

ROMAN SOCIETY

Roman society was made of two groups. Patricians were people in the rich, land-owning upper class. Plebeians were the ordinary, or regular, citizens who made up the lower class. The patricians made the laws and had most of the power, while the plebeians had very few rights.

Make The Grade

Rome had a powerful army that was very organized
and well trained. The army was made up of many
legions, or groups of soldiers.

ROME EXPANDS

The Romans soon began to conquer their neighbors, including the Etruscans in 396 BC. By 275 BC, Rome had conquered the Samnites to the north and the Greeks to the south. Rome now controlled the entire Italian **peninsula**.

ancient Roman road

Make The Grade

Beginning in 312 BC, the Romans built more than 50,000 miles (80,467 km) of road. These roads joined all of Rome and helped its army move around more easily.

Carthage was a powerful **empire** in northern Africa and southwest Europe that controlled the **Mediterranean**. Between 264 and 146 BC, Carthage and Rome fought three wars called the Punic Wars. Rome won and became the most powerful civilization in the Mediterranean.

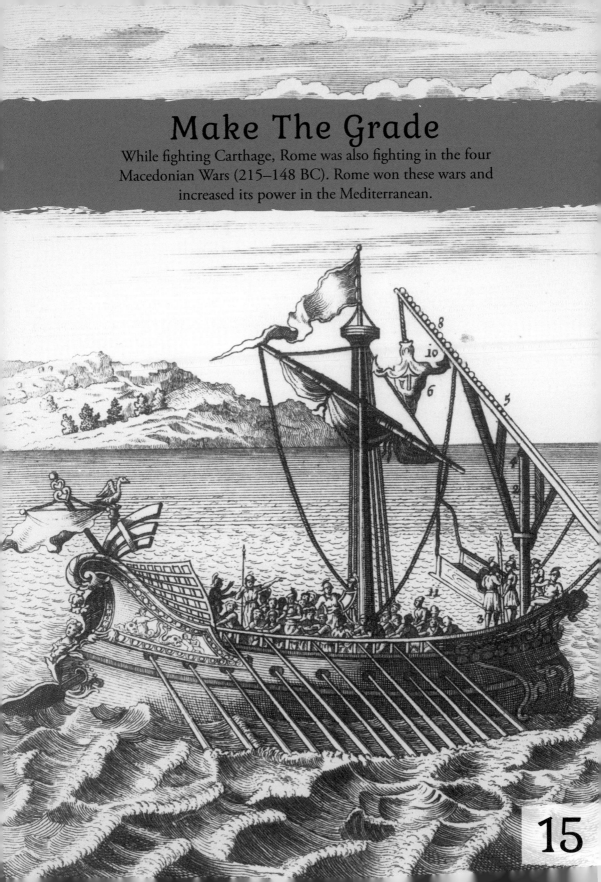

Make The Grade

While fighting Carthage, Rome was also fighting in the four Macedonian Wars (215–148 BC). Rome won these wars and increased its power in the Mediterranean.

CIVIL WARS

As Rome grew, most of the attention of the government was on the new lands instead of the people inside the republic. This led to many **civil wars** between the social classes. In 73 BC, Spartacus, a **gladiator**, led thousands of slaves in a civil war against Rome.

Make The Grade

Julius Caesar was **elected** as a consul of Rome in 60 BC. Caesar, Pompey the Great, and Marcus Crassus formed what is known today as the First Triumvirate, which is a group of three powerful ruling people.

HAIL, CAESAR!

Julius Caesar was a Roman general. Under his command northwest Europe became part of the Roman Republic. However, some members of the Senate thought Caesar was becoming too powerful. His army fought Pompey's army from 49 to 45 BC. Caesar won and was named dictator of Rome.

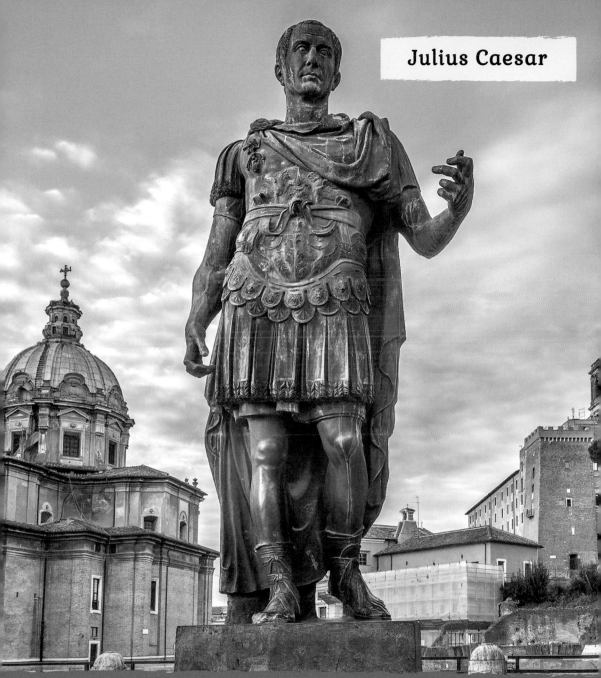

Make The Grade

Today, the word dictator means someone who rules with complete power. A Roman dictator was someone who was given complete power over the country during hard times.

C·IVLIO CAESARI

In 44 BC, Caesar was killed by members of the Senate who worried he was turning Rome into a **monarchy**. Caesar had made his grandnephew Octavian his heir, which meant Octavian would rule Rome after Caesar's death. In 31 BC, Octavian became Rome's first emperor.

Make The Grade

Octavian was given the name Augustus Caesar in 27 BC.
His rule began a 200-year-long period now called the Pax
Romana, or a time of Roman peace.

PAX ROMANA

During the Pax Romana, the empire was at its largest size. There was peace for its growing number of citizens and more time and money was spent on the arts. The Pantheon, a temple completed around AD 126, is known for its large domed, or rounded, ceiling.

Make The Grade

Early Roman religion involved many gods and goddesses. They honored these gods in buildings called temples. This lasted until about the 4th century, when Christianity became more popular.

Pantheon

BECOMING AN EMPIRE

The Roman Republic became an empire when Augustus Caesar came into power. Under Augustus Caesar and the emperors who followed, the Roman Empire grew. By AD 117, it controlled most of Europe, northern Africa, and western Asia.

EUROPE

**ROMAN EMPIRE
AD 117**

Mediterranean
Sea

AFRICA

Make The Grade

As the Roman Empire grew, the Roman culture, or beliefs
and ways of life, spread. Roman language, **politics**, law, and
architecture spread across the world.

25

DECLINE AND FALL

By AD 395, the Roman
Empire had become too big
and was split into the Western
Empire and the Eastern
Empire. The Eastern
Empire became known as
the Byzantine Empire, and
it lost much of its original
Roman culture.

Make The Grade

In AD 410, the city of Rome was destroyed by a group of **Germanic** peoples called the Visigoths. They stole Roman goods and forced many Roman citizens to leave.

Over time, the Western Empire started to weaken. Germanic tribes from the North began to attack and invade, and Roman leaders began to **abuse** their power. The Western Empire fell to Germanic tribes in AD 476. The Eastern half, though, remained strong.

Hagia Sophia, a Byzantine Empire church

Make The Grade

Over the next 200 years, Byzantine emperors tried to help the Roman people. It wasn't until the 8th century that the city of Rome finally became powerful again.

TIMELINE OF ANCIENT ROME

700s BC
Small villages near the Tiber River form a larger city that will become Rome.

c. 600 BC
Rome is conquered by the Etruscans.

509 BC
Rome becomes a republic.

c. 450 BC
The written set of laws called the Twelve Tables is created.

60 BC
The First Triumvirate is formed.

45 BC
Julius Caesar defeats Pompey and is named dictator of Rome.

44 BC
Julius Caesar is killed by Roman senators.

31 BC
Octavian (later called Augustus Caesar) becomes emperor. The Roman Empire begins.

27 BC
Pax Romana, a period of peace and growth in Rome, begins and lasts for about 200 years.

AD 395
The Roman Empire splits into the Western Empire and the Eastern, or Byzantine, Empire.

AD 476
Rome is invaded by Germanic tribes. The Western Empire falls.

GLOSSARY

abuse: to use something wrongly

architecture: a method or style of building

civil war: a war between two groups within a country

conquer: to take by force

elect: to choose for a position in a government

empire: a large area of land under the control of a single ruler called an emperor

Germanic: a term used by ancient Romans for peoples living in northern central Europe

gladiator: a man in ancient Rome who fought against another man or an animal for public entertainment

Mediterranean: a sea between Europe and Africa. Also, the area surrounding this sea.

monarchy: a government headed by a king or queen

peninsula: a piece of land that is not very wide that extends into water from the mainland

politics: the activities of the government and government officials

religion: a belief in and way of honoring a god or gods

republic: a form of government in which the people elect representatives who run the government

FOR MORE INFORMATION

BOOKS

Klar, Jeremy. *The Totally Gross History of Ancient Rome*. New York, NY: Rosen Central, 2016.

O'Connor, Jim. *Where Is the Colosseum?* New York, NY: Grosset & Dunlap, 2017.

WEBSITE

10 Facts About Ancient Rome
www.natgeokids.com/nz/discover/history/romans/10-facts-about-the-ancient-romans/#!/register
Visit this site to learn fun facts about ancient Rome.

Publisher's note to educators and parents: Our editors have carefully reviewed this website to ensure that it is suitable for students. Many websites change frequently, however, and we cannot guarantee that a site's future contents will continue to meet our high standards of quality and educational value. Be advised that students should be closely supervised whenever they access the internet.

INDEX